Affective

Jacob's Ladder

Reading Comprehension Program Social-Emotional Intelligence

Grades 4-5

Student Workbook Short Stories and Media

Joyce VanTassel-Baska, Ed.D., &
Tamra Stambaugh, Ph.D.

Routledge
Taylor & Francis Group
NEW YORK AND LONDON

First published in 2020 by Prufrock Press Inc.

Published in 2021 by Routledge
605 Third Avenue, New York, NY 10017
2 Park Square, Milton Park, Abingdon, Oxon OX14 4RN

Routledge is an imprint of the Taylor & Francis Group, an informa business.

© 2020 by Taylor & Francis Group

ISBN: 9781618219527 (pbk)

Table of Contents

The Man, the Boy, and the Donkey

By Aesop

A man and his son were once going with their Donkey to market. As they were walking along by its side a countryman passed them and said: "You fools, what is a Donkey for but to ride upon?"

So the Man put the Boy on the Donkey and they went on their way. But soon they passed a group of men, one of whom said: "See that lazy youngster, he lets his father walk while he rides."

So the Man ordered his Boy to get off, and got on himself. But they hadn't gone far when they passed two women, one of whom said to the other: "Shame on that lazy lout to let his poor little son trudge along."

Well, the Man didn't know what to do, but at last he took his Boy up before him on the Donkey. By this time they had come to the town, and the passers-by began to jeer and point at them. The Man stopped and asked what they were scoffing at. The men said: "Aren't you ashamed of yourself for overloading that poor Donkey of yours—you and your hulking son?"

The Man and Boy got off and tried to think what to do. They thought and they thought, till at last they cut down a pole, tied the Donkey's feet to it, and raised the pole and the Donkey to their shoulders. They went along amid the laughter of all who met them till they came to Market Bridge, when the Donkey, getting one of his feet loose, kicked out and caused the Boy to drop his end of the pole. In the struggle the Donkey fell over the bridge, and his fore-feet being tied together he was drowned.

"That will teach you," said an old man who had followed them:

The moral: "Please all and you will please none."

THE MAN, THE BOY, AND THE DONKEY

Facing Adversity and Challenges

F3 Rewrite the fable in a way that shows how the man and the boy could have responded in a more appropriate way to the central challenge or problem. Include a new moral that explains how to respond to the opinions of others.

Analyzing Adverse Situations and Conditions

F2 Were the challenges the man and the boy faced more internal (personal) or external (problems with other people)? What were the factors that caused the challenges?

_____

_____

_____

_____

_____

_____

_____

_____

Recognizing Adversity and Challenge

F1 What were the main challenges the man and the boy faced according to the man and the boy? According to the narrator? According to the villagers?

_____

_____

_____

_____

_____

_____

_____

THE MAN, THE BOY, AND THE DONKEY

Actualizing Potential to Advance a Goal

H3 Why is it important to remember one's purpose or goal when going about a task? Write a flash fiction piece (15 words or less with a beginning, middle, and end) or a haiku (5-syllable line, 7-syllable line, 5-syllable line) about a situation you know about when the end goal was forgotten, other influences overpowered, and the situation ended poorly. (Example: It all started well, until I listened to them; now I have stitches.)

_____

_____

_____

Understanding Roles and Affiliations

H2 How might the man have handled the suggestions of the villagers differently if he had different personality traits? What personality traits kept him from reaching his goal of getting the donkey to the market?

_____

_____

_____

Knowing Oneself

H1 It is said that our strengths are also our weaknesses. Think about the character traits of the man. What were his strengths and weaknesses, and how does he represent this statement? Make a list of your best traits. Then, think about how they might become weaknesses and list how you might prevent that situation.

_____

_____

_____

Wonder Trailer

View the official movie trailer for *Wonder*, found here: https://www.youtube.com/watch?v=ZDPEKXx_lAI.

WONDER TRAILER

Engaging in Productive Risk-Taking

G3 What is a risk you might take to make a positive difference in your life or someone else's? For example, you could sit with someone at lunch who usually eats alone or commit to ask a question in class if you don't usually talk or raise your hand. Write down what you will do and check to see that you did it within a week.

_____

_____

_____

_____

_____

Considering Multiple Perspectives

G2 When taking a risk, how might seeking someone else's perspective help you? How was that portrayed in the movie trailer? Whose perspectives matter to you and who might you talk to before taking a risk? Why?

_____

_____

_____

_____

_____

Identifying and Calculating Risks

G1 Who took the bigger risk, Auggie, or the friend who sat with him at lunch? Why do you think that?

_____

_____

_____

_____

WONDER TRAILER

Collaborating With Others

I3   Work with a partner to create a poster for an ad campaign that shows ways your schoolmates can show empathy. Provide specific examples such as "Sit with someone at lunch who is alone," "Ask someone a question about their interests," "Listen to another's perspectives," "Share an idea," etc. Use ideas from the video and other sources. Now title the poster, based on what it represents.

Communicating and Responding to Others

I2   Auggie says, "If you really want to see what people are, all you have to do is look." What does he mean? What are some ways you can "look" within yourself and at others to develop empathy?

_____

_____

_____

_____

_____

_____

_____

_____

Understanding Others' Needs and Values

I1   What are some examples of empathy (identifying with the feelings of others) shown in the movie trailer? Cite examples of how different people in the trailer showed their understanding of Auggie's needs and his value as a person.

_____

_____

_____

_____

_____

_____

_____

Music

By Arya Okten

I wriggle in my cold seat. I am bored of waiting. Then, my mother leans over and tells me to stop moving around and to be respectful. I try, I really do, but even I don't think that I succeed. Then, suddenly, as though this one thought has occupied many more moments than it should have, the woman calls my name in her high-pitched squawk. Almost immediately the pins in my feet disappear, only to be replaced by a cool sense of foreboding. I feel my mother nudge me; I have taken up too much time already. I take a gulp of air and stand up, only to have my face turn beetroot red when I see the audience staring at me. My legs take me to the front of my formidable enemy, yet friend, which is a huge black structure, made of wood, and furnished with what seems like a thousand strings. I sit on the soft leather bench, and I feel almost at home, until I feel the hundred or so pairs of eyes on my back. I take another gulp of air; it is time. My fingertips touch the edge of the smooth, hard, ivory. Beads of sweat run down my face. I am scared, but I know that in the end, I will have to face my fear. So it begins. I press the first key, then another, slowly at first, but then fast. My fingers are soon a blur, moving, and jumping like a young squirrel, but I don't care. My fingers know the routine well enough, A, G, B, and so on, but my brain is much more preoccupied. Listen, listen, that's all my brain does. Softer here, louder there, put more emotion into this part. I feel the music inside of me, pulsing, throbbing, and trying to get out. I am the pianist.

Then, all of a sudden, my song is over. My feet step lightly on the ground and after a few steps to the front of the stage my whole body bows, but in my virtual reality I am still at the piano. In my mind, I stay at the leathery seat for a few more fleeting moments, playing, but then I am back with my mother. She tells me I did great and I blush. After that the concert is a blur. I take note only of the people who played beautifully. Then, it is time to go home, but that doesn't stop me from playing. I play every day, calculating the sound of every little detail, absorbing the beautiful resonance, teaching myself how to touch the piano, so that just the right sound comes out. I will always be the pianist.

Note. Originally published in *Creative Kids* magazine, Fall 2014. Reprinted with permission by Prufrock Press.

MUSIC

Engaging in Productive Risk-Taking

G3 Write an original song, poem, or short piece like "Music" on a separate sheet of paper that tells about a time when you took a risk and how it turned out. Put it on a form of social media and comment on what it means for your audience.

Considering Multiple Perspectives

G2 How much value do you the think the pianist placed on what other people thought about the performance? What evidence in the story explains your thinking? How much value do you place on what other people think about you and your performance in a given area of endeavor? Does this ever stop you from performing? Why or why not?

_____

_____

_____

_____

_____

_____

_____

_____

Identifying and Calculating Risks

G1 What can you infer about the level of risk the pianist took to perform? Was the risk-taking necessary for the performance?

_____

_____

_____

_____

_____

_____

MUSIC

Creating a Plan for Management

J3 How might the stress management techniques after the performance have changed if the pianist had messed up? Rewrite the last paragraph of the story on a separate sheet of paper, assuming the performance did not go well, but the pianist still had a healthy response to the stressful situation.

Applying Stress Control Techniques

J2 What strategies did the pianist use to handle the stress that was felt before, during, and after the performance? What do you do? Complete the following table with examples from the text and your own experiences/example of a performance or stressful event you encountered:

Performance	Evidence From the Text	My Personal Strategies or Experiences
Before		
During		
After		

Identifying Conditions/Situations That Cause Stress

J1 What made this situation a potentially stressful one for the pianist? How do you feel before you have to get up in front of people to do something? Create a metaphor or an analogy that describes the feeling.

_____

_____

_____

Eleven

By Sandra Cisneros

View the YouTube video of Sandra Cisneros reading her story "Eleven" at https://www.youtube.com/watch?v=M_NaeodivR0.

ELEVEN

Using Emotion

E3 How could Rachel have used her emotions in a way that allowed her to have a positive voice? Create a different scenario that shows how Rachel spoke up about her sweater in a positive way. Be ready to explain how the change in Rachel's response impacts the theme of the story and Rachel's character.

_____

_____

_____

_____

_____

Expressing Emotion

E2 What do you think Rachel's 11th birthday had to do with the way she was unable to verbally express what she was feeling? What does her 11th birthday symbolize in her mind? Describe what it means to her and create an object as a symbol for her reactions.

_____

_____

_____

_____

_____

Understanding Emotion

E1 Why do you think Rachel isn't able to adequately express her emotions about the sweater and event? What evidence in the story suggests that?

_____

_____

_____

_____

_____

ELEVEN

Actualizing Potential to Advance a Goal

H3 How do Rachel's beliefs about being 11 and her responses to her experiences conflict? How might Rachel identify with her younger and older self? Make a list of her reactions and explain what her younger and older self might be saying or expecting as a response.

Reactions	Older Self	Younger Self
Example: Not being able to speak up about the sweater		

Then, write one goal from the problem in the story that you think she could work on. Be specific. What steps could she take? How will she know when she is successful?

_____

_____

Understanding Roles and Affiliations

H2 What is the central problem in this story? Who/what does Rachel want to affiliate or associate with? Why?

_____

_____

_____

Knowing Oneself

H1 Why does Rachel keep saying eleven, ten, nine, eight . . . ? What does that say about her identity?

_____

_____

_____

The Leaping Match

By Hans Christian Andersen

The flea, the grasshopper, and the frog once wanted to try which of them could jump highest; so they invited the whole world, and anybody else who liked, to come and see the grand sight. Three famous jumpers were they, as was seen by every one when they met together in the room.

"I will give my daughter to him who shall jump highest," said the King, "it would be too bad for you to have the trouble of jumping, and for us to offer you no prize."

The flea was the first to introduce himself; he had such polite manners, and bowed to the company on every side, for he was of noble blood; besides, he was accustomed to the society of man, which had been a great advantage to him.

Next came the grasshopper; he was not quite so slightly and elegantly formed as the flea; however, he knew perfectly well how to conduct himself, and wore a green uniform, which belonged to him by right of birth. Moreover, he declared himself to have sprung from a very ancient and honorable Egyptian family, and that in his present home he was very highly esteemed, so much so, indeed, that he had been taken out of the field and put into a card-house three stories high, built on purpose for him, and all of court-cards, the colored sides being turned inwards: as for the doors and windows in his house, they were cut out of the body of the Queen of Hearts. "And I can sing so well," added he, "that sixteen parlor-bred crickets, who have chirped and chirped ever since they were born and yet could never get anybody to build them a card-house, after hearing me have fretted themselves ten times thinner than ever, out of sheer envy and vexation!" Both the flea and the grasshopper knew excellently well how to make the most of themselves, and each considered himself quite an equal match for a princess.

The frog said not a word; however, it might be that he thought the more, and the house-dog, after going snuffing about him, confessed that the frog must be of a good family. And the old counselor, who in vain received three orders to hold his tongue, declared that the frog must be gifted with the spirit of prophecy, for that one could read on his back whether there was to be a severe or a mild winter, which, to be sure, is more than can be read on the back of the man who writes the weather almanac.

"Ah, I say nothing for the present!" remarked the old King, "but I observe everything, and form my own private opinion thereupon." And now the match began. The flea jumped so high that no one could see what had become of him, and so they insisted that he had not jumped at all, "which was disgraceful, after he had made such a fuss!"

The grasshopper only jumped half as high, but he jumped right into the King's face, and the King declared he was quite disgusted by his rudeness.

The frog stood still as if lost in thought; at last people fancied he did not intend to jump at all.

"I'm afraid he is ill!" said the dog; and he went snuffing at him again, when lo! all at once he made a little side-long jump into the lap of the Princess, who was sitting on a low stool close by.

Then spoke the King: "There is nothing higher than my daughter, therefore he who jumps up to her jumps highest; but only a person of good understanding would ever have thought of that, and thus the frog has shown us that he has understanding. He has brains in his head, that he has!"

And thus the frog won the Princess.

"I jumped highest for all that!" exclaimed the flea. "But it's all the same to me; let her have the stiff-legged, slimy creature, if she like him! I jumped highest, but I am too light and airy for this stupid world; the people can neither see me nor catch me; dullness and heaviness win the day with them!" And so the flea went into foreign service, where, it is said, he was killed.

And the grasshopper sat on a green bank, meditating on the world and its goings on, and at length he repeated the flea's last words—"Yes, dullness and heaviness win the day! dullness and heaviness win the day!" And then he again began singing his own peculiar, melancholy song, and it is from him that we have learnt this history; and yet, my friend, though you read it here in a printed book, it may not be perfectly true.

THE LEAPING MATCH

Engaging in Productive Risk-Taking

G3 What idea emerges from the tale about the concept of truth? What words/phrases are used to convey the writer's ideas about truth? Write a journal entry to express your thoughts and feelings about how telling the truth involves risk.

_____

_____

_____

_____

_____

Considering Multiple Perspectives

G2 How does one's perception of self and others affect his or her actions? What is the risk of being self-aware? Use evidence in the story and from your own experiences to discuss this idea.

_____

_____

_____

_____

_____

Identifying and Calculating Risks

G1 Why did the frog win the princess, according to the flea? Do you agree with that assessment? Why or why not? Assess the strengths and weaknesses of each contestant by creating a T-chart.

THE LEAPING MATCH

Collaborating With Others

I3 What does the tale provide you as a moral in how to behave? In how to relate to others? In how to accomplish what you want? Write a moral to support your ideas.

_____

_____

_____

_____

_____

_____

Communicating and Responding to Others

I2 What characteristics of the frog's behavior do you think allowed him to win the contest? With which character do you identify and why?

_____

_____

_____

_____

_____

_____

Understanding Others' Needs and Values

I1 Which jumper (frog, flea, grasshopper) best understood the needs of others? What evidence in the story supports your idea?

_____

_____

_____

_____

_____

_____

Geri's Game

Written and directed by Jan Pinkava

View the short Pixar film entitled *Geri's Game* (available online).

GERI'S GAME

Engaging in Productive Risk-Taking

G3   What skills or traits would Geri have to have in order to reach out to someone else and ask them to play chess with him? How would he approach the situation to ask someone else? What would he do if they said "no"? Create a skit of a good and bad example of how Geri might ask someone to play chess. Explain why your example is a good one.

_____

_____

_____

_____

Considering Multiple Perspectives

G2   Create a short story (with two chapters) or two monologues that portray two different perspectives of the situation—one from Geri's perspective and one from a bystander in the park who is intently staring at Geri's antics while playing chess. How do the two perspectives vary? Why do you think that is?

_____

_____

_____

_____

Identifying and Calculating Risks

G1   Why do you think Geri is playing chess by himself instead of trying to find someone to play with him? Which is riskier—reaching out to someone and possibly being rejected or being alone and being viewed as odd or unusual?

_____

_____

_____

_____

GERI'S GAME

Collaborating With Others

I3 How might collaboration with others allow for a more productive life? When is it better to work by yourself? Use Geri's example as evidence in addition to your own ideas.

_____

_____

_____

_____

_____

Communicating and Responding to Others

I2 Instead of playing chess by himself, what else might Geri have done to communicate his feelings and engage with others in productive ways? Brainstorm a list of at least 12 ways Geri might try to connect with others instead of playing chess by himself. Then select your best ideas and write a short letter to Geri suggesting some ways he might try to reach out to others.

_____

_____

_____

_____

_____

Understanding Others' Needs and Values

I1 What was Geri's problem in the story? How do you know?

_____

_____

_____

_____

_____

The Four Crafts-Men

By Jacob Grimm and Wilhelm Grimm

"Dear children," said a poor man to his four sons, "I have nothing to give you; you must go out into the wide world and try your luck. Begin by learning some craft or another, and see how you can get on." So the four brothers took their walking-sticks in their hands, and their little bundles on their shoulders, and after bidding their father good-bye, went all out at the gate together. When they had got on some way they came to four cross-ways, each leading to a different country. Then the eldest said, "Here we must part; but this day four years we will come back to this spot, and in the meantime each must try what he can do for himself."

So each brother went his way; and as the eldest was hastening on a man met him, and asked him where he was going, and what he wanted. "I am going to try my luck in the world, and should like to begin by learning some art or trade," answered he. "Then," said the man, "go with me, and I will teach you how to become the cunningest thief that ever was." "No," said the other, "that is not an honest calling, and what can one look to earn by it in the end but the gallows?" "Oh!" said the man, "you need not fear the gallows; for I will only teach you to steal what will be fair game: I meddle with nothing but what no one else can get or care anything about, and where no one can find you out." So the young man agreed to follow his trade, and he soon showed himself so clever, that nothing could escape him that he had once set his mind upon.

The second brother also met a man, who, when he found out what he was setting out upon, asked him what craft he meant to follow. "I do not know yet," said he. "Then come with me, and be a star-gazer. It is a noble art, for nothing can be hidden from you, when once you understand the stars." The plan pleased him much, and he soon became such a skillful star-gazer, that when he had served out his time, and wanted to leave his master, he gave him a glass, and said, "With this you can see all that is passing in the sky and on earth, and nothing can be hidden from you."

The third brother met a huntsman, who took him with him, and taught him so well all that belonged to hunting, that he became very clever in the craft of the woods; and when he left his master he gave him a bow, and said, "Whatever you shoot at with this bow you will be sure to hit."

The youngest brother likewise met a man who asked him what he wished to do. "Would not you like," said he, "to be a tailor?" "Oh, no!" said the young man; "sitting cross-legged from morning to night, working back-wards and forwards with a needle and goose, will never suit me." "Oh!"

answered the man, "that is not my sort of tailoring; come with me, and you will learn quite another kind of craft from that." Not knowing what better to do, he came into the plan, and learnt tailoring from the beginning; and when he left his master, he gave him a needle, and said, "you can sew anything with this, be it as soft as an egg or as hard as steel; and the joint will be so fine that no seam will be seen."

After the space of four years, at the time agreed upon, the four brothers met at the four cross-roads; and having welcomed each other, set off towards their father's home, where they told him all that had happened to them, and how each had learned some craft.

Then, one day, as they were sitting before the house under a very high tree, the father said, "I should like to try what each of you can do in this way." So he looked up, and said to the second son, "At the top of this tree there is a chaffinch's nest; tell me how many eggs there are in it." The stargazer took his glass, looked up, and said, "Five." "Now," said the father to the eldest son, "take away the eggs without letting the bird that is sitting upon them and hatching them know anything of what you are doing." So the cunning thief climbed up the tree, and brought away to his father the five eggs from under the bird; and it never saw or felt what he was doing, but kept sitting on at its ease. Then the father took the eggs, and put one on each corner of the table, and the fifth in the middle; and said to the huntsman, "Cut all the eggs in two pieces at one shot." The huntsman took up his bow, and at one shot struck all the five eggs as his father wished. "Now comes your turn," said he to the young tailor; "sew the eggs and the young birds in them together again, so neatly that the shot shall have done them no harm." Then the tailor took his needle, and sewed the eggs as he was told; and when he had done, the thief was sent to take them back to the nest, and put them under the bird without its knowing it. Then she went on sitting, and hatched them: and in a few days they crawled out, and had only a little red streak across their necks, where the tailor had sewn them together.

"Well done, sons!" said the old man: "you have made good use of your time, and learnt something worth the knowing; but I am sure I do not know which ought to have the prize. Oh! that a time might soon come for you to turn your skill to some account!"

Not long after this there was a great bustle in the country; for the king's daughter had been carried off by a mighty dragon, and the king mourned over his loss day and night, and made it known that whoever brought her back to him should have her for a wife. Then the four brothers said to each other, "Here is a chance for us; let us try what we can do." And they agreed to see whether they could not set the princess free. "I will soon find out where she is, however," said the star-gazer, as he looked through his glass: and he soon cried out, "I see her afar off, sitting upon a rock in the sea; and I can spy the dragon close by, guarding her." Then he went to the king, and asked for a ship for himself and his brothers; and they sailed together over the sea, till they came to the right place. There they found the princess sitting, as the star-gazer had said, on the rock; and the dragon was lying asleep, with his head upon her lap. "I dare not shoot at him," said the huntsman, "for I should kill the beautiful young lady also." "Then I will try my skill," said the thief; and went and stole her away from under the dragon, so quietly and gently that the beast did not know it, but went on snoring.

Then away they hastened with her full of joy in their boat towards the ship; but soon came the dragon roaring behind them through the air; for he awoke and missed the princess. But when he got over the boat, and wanted to pounce upon them and carry off the princess, the huntsman took up his bow and shot him straight through the heart, so that he fell down dead. They were still not safe; for he was such a great beast that in his fall he overset the boat, and they had to swim in the open sea upon a few planks. So the tailor took his needle, and with a few large stitches put some of the planks together; and he sat down upon these, and sailed about and gathered up all the pieces of the boat; and then tacked them together so quickly that the boat was soon ready, and they then reached the ship and got home safe.

When they had brought home the princess to her father, there was great rejoicing; and he said to the four brothers, "One of you shall marry her, but you must settle amongst yourselves which it is to be." Then there arose a quarrel between them; and the star-gazer said, "If I had not found the princess out, all your skill would have been of no use; therefore she ought to be my wife." "Your seeing her would have been of no use," said the thief, "if I had not taken her away from the dragon; therefore she ought to be my wife." "No, she is my beloved," said the huntsman; "for if I had not killed the dragon, he would, after all, have torn you and the princess into pieces." "And if I had not sewn the boat together again," said the tailor, "you would all have been drowned; therefore she is to be my wife." Then the king put in a word, and said, "Each of you is right; and as all cannot marry the young lady, the best way is for neither of you to have her hand in marriage: for the truth is, there is somebody she likes a great deal better. But to make up for your loss, I will give each of you, as a reward for his skill, half a kingdom." So the brothers agreed that this plan would be much better than either quarrelling or marrying a lady who had no mind to have them. And the king then gave to each half a kingdom, as he had said; and they lived very happily the rest of their days, and took good care of their father; and somebody took better care of the young lady, than to let either the dragon or one of the Crafts-men marry her.

THE FOUR CRAFTS-MEN

Collaborating With Others

I3 Create a moral for the story about the relationship between collaboration and success, using the craftsmen's collective feats as evidence. Apply your moral to your own life. How have you collaborated with others to bring about a greater good?

_____

_____

_____

_____

_____

Communicating and Responding to Others

I2 The princess is rescued because the craftsmen express empathy for her situation. How do they demonstrate their feelings? Does the ending of the story show empathy or greed? What makes you think that? What examples of empathy have you illustrated in your life?

_____

_____

_____

_____

_____

Understanding Others' Needs and Values

I1 What were the needs of the craftsmen in the story? What about the princess? The father? The king?

_____

_____

_____

_____

_____

THE FOUR CRAFTS-MEN

Reflecting on Patterns of Achievement

K3 What accomplishments have meant the most to you so far in life? What processes and strategies did you use to reach your goal? Create a blueprint of your road to success by writing down the plan that has worked for you.

_____

_____

_____

_____

_____

Assessing Strengths and Interests

K2 How did the brothers meet their goal of becoming proficient in a craft? What skills did they practice?

_____

_____

_____

_____

_____

Identifying Barriers to Achievement

K1 What barriers did the brothers encounter as they tried to become proficient at a craft? What strategies did they use to overcome them?

_____

_____

_____

_____

_____

Piper

Written and directed by Alan Barillaro

View the short Pixar film entitled *Piper* (available online).

PIPER

Facing Adversity and Challenges

F3   Create a character that provides a monologue on how to handle adversity based on what you learned from the video. Which ideas are most important to stress and why?

_____

_____

_____

Analyzing Adverse Situations and Conditions

F2   What strategies and personal characteristics did the bird employ to overcome the challenges it faced? How might you apply these same strategies and personal characteristics to help you overcome an adverse situation or challenge in your life? Complete a 3-column chart like the one below on a separate sheet of paper.

Bird's Personal Characteristics	Strategies the Bird Employs	Situations in Your Life

Recognizing Adversity and Challenge

F1   Create a list on a separate sheet of paper of the figurative and literal problems the bird faced. Look through your list and compare it with a classmate's list. Together, discuss the following question: What was the main problem the bird had to face? Explain your thinking, using evidence from the video.

PIPER

Engaging in Productive Risk-Taking

G3 How might one's emotions be a help or hindrance when taking a risk? Write a lesson or set of rules that might help someone else decide when he or she should give in to fears because it is an unsafe choice versus when he or she should push through fears and overcome obstacles. Use examples from your life, conversations with your family, other books you have read, and the video to help you write your response.

Considering Multiple Perspectives

G2 How did the bird's observance of other perspectives help it manage the risks it faced? Look at your plot map from G1. What do you notice about the emotions the bird might have been feeling before and after considering multiple perspectives?

_____

_____

_____

_____

_____

_____

Identifying and Calculating Risks

G1 Create a plot map of important events and actions of the young bird's life. Label the emotions you think the bird was feeling as a result of each action (or risk) in the video.